For Generations to go backwards

*Whenever I think of not publishing
youth comes to mind,
and how this saved me from drowning
when I was young.*

*I also think of a young drunken in the maken'
to be something,*

*maybe*

*– who likes to read my stuff*

Lilijanea J.

# Go Backwards

## *so they won't see you*

*series: Words that can be spoken out Loud*

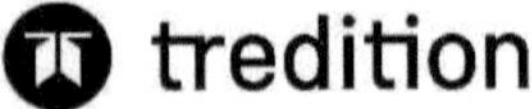
tredition

# Inhaltsverzeichnis

## Let me paint you a picture

*Der Horizont war blau*

    *nach so vielen Tagen des Regens*

*24 ganze Stunden*

    *doch jetzt zeigt sich die Sonne*

*verabschiedet sich    von mir    allein*

*denn ich bin hier, richtig?*

*Vor mir die Baumkronen   entzücken in Farbe*

*eine klare Linie zeichnet sich ab*

*von den in Nacht eintauchenden Blättern.*

*Welch Spektakel  nur für meine Augen*

*Es wahr*

*nur für mich?    richtig?*


                        *in diesem Moment*

*ich drehe die Sicht*

        *hinter mir das helle Licht der Sonne*

*das Gelb,*

            *das Weiß,*

                    *das Rot*

                        *und das Lila-Rosa*

*sie alle brennen im Blau        so leuchtend*

*;*

*ich setze einen Fuß zurück*

                *einen nach vorne –*

*zerrissen  nun  vom Spektakel*

*lechzend nach den besten Plätzen*

*Im Spiegel des Hauses gar um die Ecke blickend*

spiegelt sich der Horizont erneut

welch wundersame Tafel

gibt mir das Gefühl vom Strand

vom weiten Ozean.

Ich luur an den Häusern vorbei

denke an die Wiese dahinter,

das saftige Gras und die mich kitzelnden Hälmer


Es ist nur eine Erinnerung,

doch ist sie so schön

sie reicht mir

bis ins Herz hinein ein Gemeinssamsein

im Untergang des Sonnenscheins.

Und ich drehe halb,

wie der Mond an diesem Tage

erneut flimmern die letzten Farben des Tages

in den Wipfeln des Waldes

wie ruhig liegt die Seele

 in all ihren Namen

# 2024

How conflicted the mind s et . How very fragile the art is of fragmenting light . How foolish to ask and how devastating to fold.

The force of strength of doubt seems as rooted as the force of matter and motivation. I for once wouldn't speak the truth if I tell you the separation exists.

In my essence lies the question and the attempt, for the answer lies not in my words but don't be misguided by forces that tell you they are not there.

However they are not told

it's still all there.

All that you need

# Young Existentialism

I

Es gibt nichts Gutes und nichts Böses

*erst meine Gedanken machen es dazu*

Ich möchte Tattoos wie Bilder

als Memento

weil ich diese Bilder nie vergessen will


Sie zu stechen in mein Fleisch

sie werden Lebensaufgaben sein

Como que no tienes energía?

A veces tienes energía positiva

a veces negativa

Trabajemos en convertirla

Lilijanea J.

Das Herz braucht keine Überbegriffe

keine Zäune

der Kopf benutzt sie

um das Herz

besser zu verstehn'


Sie zu beschreiben zu können

erfassen wir sie.

Doch das Herz muss nur offen sein

um zu sehen

mit dem Kopf entscheiden wir es zu öffnen

es zu schließen


Wir brauchen den Kopf

um zuzuhören

um zu erfassen

um zu verstehen


Ich bin auf dem richtigen Weg


So befreie ich mich von der Angst


den falschen Weg zu gehen

denn es ist meiner


Ich möchte ihn nur selbst wählen

keinen Gewählten gehen

Ich möchte mein Herz nicht verschließen

weil ich einen ungeschriebenen Weg begehe

von dem ich nicht abzukommen gedenke


Ich bin nicht Gott

ich weiß nicht wohin mich mein Weg führt

Ich habe genug damit zu tun

zu akzeptieren was ist

als das ich mich damit beschäftigen könnte

was sein wird

*eventuell*

Ich fürchte

sie glauben lieber denen

die ihnen Angst machen


Momo-

Bewared die Liebe

zum Leben gewiss

dann komme die Liebe & Güte

*vom HerrGott gewiss*

Warum gibt Kontrolle Sicherheit

& Freiheit macht Angst?

# Money is safety

we like to feel safe

I like to feel safe

We can't live completely without it

not in society

because when we do so

we are

dependent on others

I like independency

You can't be independent without money,

Can you?

**Money is a disease**

and we created it

# Wider

I don't regret how I lived the las decades

I just don't want to close my eyes

from what I see know


I don't think my look changed

I think its way wider now

Das ganze Leben besteht aus Phasen

jede einzelne ist wichtig

wie die andere

Solo podemos entender los que está dentro

de nuestra conciencia

Si un momento ya es hermoso

porque desear más siempre?

**Wann hört** deine **Liebe auf und wann fängt**

mein **Besitzdenken an?**

# The culture of boxes

They go from box to box

out of their box in the morning

into another box

to get into another box

and when they die

they go into a box

to put it under the earth

They are crazy about boxes

They don't know anything

about the sun

## Mut zum Leben

Versteckt in all den Schatten

hinterm Alltag sicher gefang'

finde ich das letzte Bisschen,

das ich weiß.

Gezeiten sind vergangen

doch die Stille flüstert weiter

von nah, von fern,

noch gerade scheint schon so weit weg


Kennen wir's nicht alle?


Verfolgt von all dem Schmerz

stehen wir uns selbst meist im Weg

den Mut zu ergreifen

zu lachen und zu strahlen

von nah, von fern,

so nah

noch gerade scheint schon so weit weg

Ich werde gegen all die Regeln

da stehn' und singend sie besiegen

ich werde lieben, kämpfen, siegen

ich will leben,

Leben

leben

Leben

leben

# Gospel

If you don't bring out what is within you

it might kill you

if you bring out what is within you

it will safe you

# Trigger Angst

Die Inneren Ängste aus der Vergangenheit

Die Angst

dass mir dasselbe widerfährt

was mich damals zu Boden gerissen hat


Die Angst davor

so schwach zu sein

wie man es schon einmal war


Die Angst davor

zu versagen

zu fallen


Verlust.angst

Die Angst

stehen zu bleiben

Trigger

Angst

## **Just a flower**

If I was just a flower in the wind

I would let the breeze touch my skin

If I was just a tiger in the woods

Oh, would I be content,

So tell me if I couldn't

Tell me is it possible to go?

So far from here,

far from home

from everything I've been told


Or if I could just run away backwards

there where the grass is still green

beings care and people still talk

without having a gun beside

and without hearing the poor ones cry


Well I don't have to run away

its my choice to stay

and build up what was broke

Yes, we create the system with our hands

Go Backwards

Go Backwards

# Active Thought

41

# II

## Intentions set

I finally found

the balance

in art

 to communicate

with you

.I do – not shall


this lucha

which never finds its end.


Sometimes

I urge the need for a home

and others I will be gone

home –

If I don't move

the fragile sound

of my voice

can't be heard

in time

who has to grow

out of their stagnation

so called comfort zone


I inherited

the name

nun–payable

I am not refundable

I gain

confidence

whenever I am on the run

to give you notice

to push you from being done

to try it again

.

and again

and again

I know

there will be no liberation

no satisfaction

for me

if I am not honest

and if I don't touch you

within


I am here to serve

I am here to give testimony to the followed

I am fighting demons

inside

they feed off my ignorance

they count on my laziness

incompetence

to declutter my brain

in the fogginess


between my Armour

that shines

and the bright cloudy haze

in steam mist

that chases me

I lurk tired and continuously


while          culture

dominantly continuous

to bother me

with non-sense of

comfortability

not seeing none-sense

not degenerating superiority

my confidence is stacked

by this


I choose

to be bothered by this

this culture

doesn't represent my nature

it is irritating as it ships

ruled the word

in confidence


This already happened,

hasn't it?

So, it was

so it is


what will be?


Parameters of normality

questioning the status quo

within the Capitol

I am done pleasing

it's only feeding

more noise

so

greedy

so,

try me


I don't mind the scare

I accept being ruled by

I will dismantle the rules by


I am

done

thinking

I am

done

hoping

I am

doing


I am all alone

with this

until I am not.


It has n.o.t always been done that way

popularity

won't bring anything

as an attitude


I have seen

there is

people

who have faith in their believe


and

siehe da

released

unity and grieve

I am about to bundle

the sparks known to be

around the world

we are all alone?

No,

we are million

not waiting in a cage

to be saved

by a system


but known to grow strong

from a place

no domination of an ongoing

murder and suppression


the tables are about to turn

just close your eyes and imagine

no one can touch this

for change we are born

# Poetry Slam

You got to

stop

repressing your magic

don't limit yourself to

whatever

somebody thinks

you should do.


If it's not your calling

don't wait too long

cause the dice is rolling.

Yeah, the minute

you start pushing

away your comfort zone

it starts pushing back.


So, hold on to your cour

meant by heart

-age with greatness,


so start drinking your wisdom

& you find the bliss of winning

since you


learned that courage

it takes

doing without trying to get

rid of fearing


accepting, that you'll be afraid

yeah, could even really be failing

ones and twice


but

you'll do it anyway


and help me say

defining failing is actually up to you

that nobody chooses but you

which are your goals in life


which lessons your soul has to undertake

that, nobody feels but yourself

to find the answers you are

sometimes still looking for


& choose your own imaginary land

You pick to be brave

& helpful & friendly

but fair to yourself, don't


let nobody get in your way

when, you are just going your path

and someone wants to steal your essence

or takes a chance on pissing you off


for the sake of pissing you off.

Yes, sharing & being humble

without getting ripped off

is an art of strolling


especially

when suspicious looks

are following your back

try holding me back


it is

difficult to understand

if you lose your time

where is a lack of respect


self–respect

is one of the essential goals

in life it is

sharing like loving

are universal codes

that the sharers understand

by feelings

not by being told


but the ones who are not sharing

just taking

feeding themselves off

breathing in to smock


they will be bearing

their comfort zone

when, too late they realized

they created their world

their comfort

on the outside

to bright

in their eyes


shined the golden prize


while the sharers,

the barrier breakers,

*always*

the first ones to wake up

inside

.


for a long time

are built

the tunnels of the cribs

in the valley

of my hips


what amazingly

for those

still unaware

not living there

unprepared

looks like nothing

but a maze


You better start

those lessons of yours

to learn.

## Earth tells

The ways

of self discovery

are bolt


In a way

wings

appeared

and still roots arise

holding me

as teaching tells

down to earth

# Hannah Arendt

& no bubble

shall ever be enough

tempting means stall

for as Hannah said

it is dangerous for all

Me only want to be able to love me

love is liberation

including without excluding

is my truth that has to be lived

is to materialize our truths

for our goal should be to see

then someone else can see

it is not

possible

until

it is

.

for this remembering

being alone will be the most connecting

resurrection

of

humanity is necessity

# "You deserve this"

I got this voice in my head

telling me, that I am special

shackles

I hear these whisperer inside

showing me the difference

shackles

Oh, tell me

I deserve this

shackles

whisper

I got to

I got to

run away from this pain

[I deserve this]

It has to stop this shame

[I deserve this]

Oh this shame

[I deserve this]

[they tell me, I deserve this]

I want to

blame

.you.

Someone.

Make it stop

I feel so much sadness,

it shadows my trust

my love

you hurt

&

I love you so much.


Enough

I want to learn

how to protect

Enough

# Homage

Oh sun,

when you wake up

pitched our voices

amazed

wake our heads


once your light meets our eyes

through the window

bright

Is it because you meet god herself?

Before she goes to sleep

Or is it because you shake the faith

of our new day out of your sleeves.

## Masse ohne Platz

*Gäbest du mir keinen Platz,*

*Oh,was würde mit dem Sonnenaufgang?*

*Wärest du einfach da*

*in jedem Takt*

*geschähe jeder Tag*

*ohne Nuancen,*

*ohne Chancen,*

*je*

*deinen Namen zu erkennen.*

# Don't

Give in

rest low

= this should lift you up =

*Don't be this*
*Don't touch that*

Baby, are you coming?

I am out,

I stopped bottling it up

I dare to be proud

I figured out

I can decide to stop.


If you don't have a perspective

you can't really see it through

It's hard being what you cant see

it's harder trying to be what you shall not

So let it _

be what you feel

feel free.


They try to hold

the powerful down

I am here to bring you up


One step at a time

It's never the peek

heal hides

only in the climb

When you have to walk

the extra mile

to get somewhere

& you find joy

allow yourself

to enjoy the ride

that hurtful pain

you'd learn

to accept.


Like there is no sun

without the moon

Dance into the spheres


in between.


You've always been

a sunset girl

so be brave enough

to let out the sunrise boy


Trust in the process

it leads you to truth

without blame shaming

without being rude


unnecessarily

causing a scene

of attention

for uninvited people


lack of self control


giving power to people

doesn't bring out the best

Have you seen that?


So,

if you want to chanel

your original

don't duplicate

work the traumas of your past


blood


victom

s ized offenders


blood


vic

torion defenders

# **Runnin'**

is it possible

to let your past go

I don't know

honestly

I don't think so

But the spaces

if you except yourself

allow you

to be your very own

# Illusions

I said

be aware of illusions

when you

want to believe

something

but the reality

is not that fancy at all


While

your mind is running

wild with thoughts

simplicity goes by.


Wouldn't it be enough?

Reality

in all it's flaw fullness

It is there

always

if you want

it

and not.


Everything

is

everything

even if you hold on

to only

one

thing

# Yin

the moon


There is a voice inside of you

What does it say?


The window is a bit open,

so the birds flew in.

They used every gap they could find

se aprovecharon

de cada rinconcito

abierto por el viento.

Había qu sellar

la ventana con pegamento

porque entraron y me quitaron el pan

Lo arrancaron de mis manos

lo picaron de mi cabello

Lo arrancaron con toda fuerza

Madre mía que violencia

# Mercedes Sosa

## *cancion de las simples cosas*

una se despide

insensiblemente

de pequenas cosas

lo mismo que un árbol

que en tiempo de otoño

se queda sin hojas


al fin la tristeza

es la muerte lenta

de las simples cosas

y esas cosas simples

que quedan doliendo

en el corazón


Una vuelve siempre

a los viejos sitios

donde amó la vida

y entonces comprende

cómo están ausentes

las cosas queridas


Por eso muchacha

no partas ahora

sonando el regreso

que el amor es simple

y las cosas simples

las devora el tiempo

una vuelve siempre

a los viejos sitios

donde amó la vida

**Lied der einfachen Dinge**

Gesichert sind

die unsensiblen

Verabschiedungen

von den einfachen Dingen

so wie ein Baum

der in der Herbstzeit

ohne Blätter weilt


Letzten Endes

ist die Traurigkeit

der langsame Tod

der einfachen Dinge

und diese einfachen Dinge

die schmerzend zurückbleiben

im Herzen


Gesichert ist

Die stetige Rückkehr

an die alten Orte

wo das Leben geliebt wurde

und dann das Verständnis

über das Fehlen

der geliebten Dinge


Deshalb, mein Junge

gehe nicht jetzt

deine Rückkehr ersehnend

Die Liebe ist einfach

und die einfachen Dinge

werden von der Zeit zerstreut


Bleib hier

im strahlendsten Licht

dieses Mittags

Hier, wo das Brot in der Sonne liegt,

findest du

einen gedeckten Tisch

Deshalb, mein Junge

gehe nicht jetzt

deine Rückkehr ersehnend

Die Liebe ist einfach

und die einfachen Dinge

werden von der Zeit zerstreut


Gesichert ist die Rückkehr

zu den alten Orten

wo das Leben geliebt wurde

# Schreibsamkeit

Im Streben nach Einsamkeit

Im Streben nach ihr.

Ich suhle, ich winde mich

Nach Innen

hin, zu ihr, ich erfreue mich in dir

Glücksehlig

bis zur Einsamkeit.

Ich strebe nach dir

nach Außen

Welt

du,

die die Fülle auslebt

wie ich einst

mit gewülstetem Bauch

in Erinnerungen schwelgend

gelüstet mein Herz nach companía

# Re bound

Wir

er

nähern uns

lustvoll,

wir

 zwei zerbrochene Scherben

einer Teekanne,

die

einst meine Seele erwärmte

# AQUÍ ESTOY

Jr arenivas

Le temo a la mujer en la que me voy

convirtiendo, porque es la que sabe tejer y

destejer realidades, porque es la que deja

de idealizar para empezar a caminar...

Porque siempre quise que todo sea hermoso

y perfecto, color frambuesa, olor lavanda,

sonrisa de miel, y no hacía más que atascar

en mi garganta las lágrimas, los me duele,

los basta...

Y hoy, viene la anciana que un día seré y

me dice que todo está bien, y sigo respiran-

do...

Me está creciendo nueva piel, una piel más

fuerte, más buitre, más halcón, más sabia,

más honesta, brutalmente honesta, y tam-

bién

más solitaria, y por ello amo más genuina-

mente...

Yo soñaba con cosas imposibles, y no, no

reniego de mis sueños ni de lo imposible,

tan sólo que me cansé de buscar lo imposible

por temor a lo posible...

Hoy sé que también soy tierra, y también

soy ciclo, y ya no anhelo un mundo que aún

no

existe...

Lo que anhelo es sentir mi sangre recorrer

el paisaje que me viste y desviste, hacer el

amor conmigo mismo, con el viento y con el

mar,

inhalar y exhalar consciente, tomar la vida

que

ya está y empezar a caminar...

Puedo abrazar lo que soy, ese abrazo soñado

y rezado por siglos, aquí estoy, siendo lo que

soy...

A lo más hermoso de la creación,

en especial a una tapatía...

Jr arenivas

– Jesús Quintero: "Señor Gala, ¿qué es lo más inteligente que se puede hacer en esta vida?"

– Antonio Gala: "En principio yo le diría: irse a una playa. Pero en el fondo, de verdad, tengo que decirle que salir de esta especie de laberinto en que nos han metido, una vida que no es la nuestra y que no es la mandada. Que es una organización que necesita esclavos para seguir manteniendo la pura organización que necesita esclavos, y así hasta el final. Salirse de esa cadena terrible, desencadenarse. A riesgo

de la soledad, a riesgo de la falta de compren-
sión, pero irse un poco al campo, en el mejor de
los sentidos. Salir de esa

extraña y monótona esclavitud de cada día.
Darle a cada día su propio afán, pero también
su propia sonrisa, su propio gozo, su propio color, su propio aroma. Eso es la inteligencia.
Porque una inteligencia que no nos ayude a vivir, no la quiero. No me sirve para nada. No
creo que le sirva para nada a nadie".

# By the river


I remember the constellation

of the moon

when you brought

stars down

talking about

freedom

of truth

as prove, as artifacts they served you

well,

I was still running around looking for truth

Now sitting by the

water that cleanse me

seeing the most beautiful flowers

I think of the fortune

If to get everything

you have to be careful

what you wish for

## By the lake

In times like these

peace

lies in the space

beyond suffering

Still I'll go back

My duties I must fulfill

I can't turn

my back on mundanity



*like someone once said*

*they would have to*

*come get me*

*out of the woods*

*I still got words to say*

## Nombrada

Con esta cara nací

Esta cara la llevo

desde que mi madre me parió

Cambió por temporadas

con fuerza externa al teñirla

Aber der Antlitz

el mismo más o meno

Este cuerpecito mío

aunque me dicen ahora mujer

por las caderas que me crecieron

yo lo trato igual que el

que me dió luz mi madre

hace tanto tiempo


Dicho es

me sentí

fea

me sentí

hermosa

desgastada

y

fresca

como saliendo recién del mar querido

vivo y saludable

como frágil y sin fuerza

Cambié tanto

la imagen

mirando al espejo

interiorizando

o sea

cambiando mis adentros

cambiando el yo

por como me mira la gente

dependi**é**ndolo de mi estado de **á**nimo

por causas solamente externas

que ahora me parece de sobra

mi apariencia f**í**sica

*casi?*

## Ten cuidado what you wish for

Me crees,

será marcito

que dejando que importe

ella

se me cae

un peso y daré paso

a que tomen

espacio

el carino

Hasta cuando estés

Y si te tengo que dejar

*toda aspiración*

## Eine dieser Schreibe Menschen

die den Stift nicht weglegen kann

mürrisch

gelenkt

von Intuition & Intellekt

die alles auseinandernehmen kann muss

schwer beschäftigt

zu begreifen

die Teile im Leben wieder zusammenzusetzen

um nicht den Weg zur Realität

*zu verlieren*

Wo für den einen die Kunst ist

etwas eigenes zu kreieren

bedeutet die Kunst für die Kreativen

nicht den Bezug zur Rationalität zu verlie-

ren

Im Glück gebettet

verstanden zu haben

Zweiteres in den Augen zu tragen

Lege ich das Schwert zu Boden

und statt gegen sich selbst zu kämpfen

frage ich mich nun, ist es möglich

trotz dem Glück im Gegenwärtigen zu su-

chen

ich meine Fern ab

von meiner Fantasie

wo Menschen weilen

die

ich nicht kontrollieren mag

Menschen, die ich gerne mag

und doch so fürchte

sind es sie

die

mich fürchten lassen

die mich abweisen und

auf mich traten, man lehrte mich

sie, die Menschen wollen immer etwas ha-

ben

Vertraue ich, liebe ich, ohne Agenda, ja was

soll dann daraus werden

aus meinem Nichts-Haben-Wollenden sein;

aus meinen Fragen?

Was bringt es zu lieben, wissend es geht um

nichts,

als um des Liebenswillen Namen zu sagen

*Menschen bereiten mir Unbehagen*

# Cristobalizado

Acabo

de descubrir

que el tuyo

es el ombligo

del tercer

mundo

**Efraín Huerta**

## Kolumbusiert

Ich habe

soeben

entdeckt

der deine ist

der Nabel

der dritten Welt

# Reisen im Reise Zeitalter

Sie reisen sehr viel

doch sehen Sie was?

Was sehen Sie?

Sehen Sie

*Anderes*

Oder macht aus Ihnen

das andere

Etwas anders?

Leben Sie

wie

Andere

Urlauben

4 Mal im Jahr

wo Anders?

## Stehen Geblieben

Wir

er

leben

das Gleiche

und doch könnte es

anders nicht sein.

Die Aussage

immer die Selbe

'Ich solls doch nicht so eng sehn'

'Wie sollte es anders auch sein?'

Ich wollte dir einmal meine Augen reichen

du siehest die meinen Tausenden, die mich

begleiten

so viel Stärke liegt darin,

dass du trotzdem bist

auch wenn du Etwas anderes siehst

Lilijanea J.

# Hemmung

Wären wir alle

gemeinsam

einsam

könnten

wir der Angst

vor der Ungewissheit

in die Augen blicken voll Hoffnung

in Würde sähen für dich, für sie, für mich

Doch sitze ich

mit Zorn im Rachen

des leblosen Drachenmauls

und muss mich täglich fragen

was das soll, was ich soll

ich kämpfe

leise

im Herzen

Weichen

um

stellen

von eigenen

Feindbildern

umgeben

Jeder hier

hegt

einen

Groll

Zu gehen ist schwer

zurÜckzukommen schwerer

# All' Tag

Und wenn jeder seinen All tag beginnt

die neue Woche gerinnt

überkommt es mich aufs Neue

mein Weg führt mich weg

weg aus der Stadt

schnell

?

weg von dieser schnellliebigen Gesellschaft

## Wenn es Zeit ist zu gehen

Ich liebe es zu teilen

& kann ich das nur

wenn ich etwas habe

Hier verliere ich mehr

als ich gewinnen kann

wenn ich bleibe

# Free ing

121

# III

# Modern Realism

You don't have to imagine a macondo

You see the rivers' bed of death stream to-

wards the capitol

See her daughters

slaughtered

In their underwear

In cemeteries

recycled

Church girls

Without a purpose


And then you stand

In front of ho chi minh

Like a french

Frie

Like US

Eating bánh mì

This side of colonialism

Its birth is modernism

and it sits behind the taxis' shelf

Waiting for the come and go

The once white shell not care

For with their means is paid the prize

Of a return ticket


But


What you gonna do

When they come for you?

# Y ou & the y

Because the y

Exist

Only

When you insist

In you

Being an ignorant fool

Of Self

In deep in

Modern

Colonial

Dominant

Supreme

You

Are normal

Are the status quo

You

Don't ask your Self

You

Don't have to ask your Self

You exist in all spheres

You

Don't leave space

for anything else

You know everything


You bet


nothing is going to change

You bet on your comfort

You don't want change

You want your comfort

You don't want to give

anything

To those,

Who are not You

That is how You become a they

an alien to ally

an ally to alien

This de-humanising is de-humanising

You r self

You can't see that

So, your Self must die

# Rodinha

Хорошо мать

Я тебя вижу

Двигаюсь в твоём путь

# En contra

Me pregunto

porque estoy en contra

más mi boca no se abre


Te ví a ti

en tu silueta de buena

me recuerdas a mi


Te vendes

por fama

te dejas vencer

por el miedo


Si fuera tan fácil

amiga


yo hubiera ido contigo


Pero me quedo atrás

sabiendo bien

lo que hago


yo veramente

no anhelo la fama

quiero paz

quiero suenos


y así quedarme tranquila

aunque nunca lo logro

aprendo la capacidad

de que el éxito

seré yo

# espacio seguro

Hay una cosa más importante

que la atracción que atraes

y esta es el respeto

que si no lo tienes

desvanece


Yo no creo en la iglesia,

pero creo en tu mirada

en ella veo mi dios

en el veo mi diosa

.

Toda casa que da espacio

a que el y ella entren

con permiso me quedo

con permiso

vuelvo

# si las paredes fueran transparentes

Las paredes de afuera

de la casa nunca cuentan

el cariño o la falta

de amor

que se halla dentro


por eso gracias

por recordarme

lo que es importante

en esta vida será

la luz de camino en adelante

## La naturaleza

se hace nuestra compañía

Somos la tierra

el agua

la luz

las plantas

los animales

la casa común

de la familia

Por el camino frente a los poderes

que marginan

nos hacemos proximidad del prójimo

que necesitará nuestro aceite

de ternura

nuestros brazos

de solidaridad

no hay más camino que la amistad

**Ernesto**

## For all the people

who think in doubts

It doesn't matter what your rhythm is

or what instrument you play

if you have something to say

express it in a rhythmic way

# Your fear is too easy

In a society

where variety

saved me

in a circle

freed

in a postwar

germany

my reality

is a migration country

How come

it has passed a century

and still fear can be spread



about migration

and refugees

?

Your fear of me?

You fear for me?

You decide my fear for me?

You fear of freedom

on a sign

it's too easy

since when

comes freedom

from having to chose

a men-made side?

# Walk it through

Birth and family

presented to me

was never what only determined me

When I close my eyes

I can feel the whole world around me

Born on the steps

I walked up and down

to see what's next

Always wanted more

forget keeping score

only scars



I dare honesty

I dare to grow

out of colonial thought

I dare my family

I dare the police

state

I dare myself

I dare everyone around me

Honestly

A life is nothing

if not

holding on

and staying true

to your believes

its nothing

written

on a piece of paper

if not felt

hold high

and fought for

It doesn't matter where your from

it only matters where you at

# Miss y

Would you forget who you are?

Cause if they roll me a carpet

You make damn sure

to create a space

for the crowd

that rooted for you

the steps you swing to

the rhythm in you do shine

the masters that showed you how

don't forget to be humble, you share, you

care,

on your own, you know you'll never be alo-

ne, you'll see

# She reflection in mine

You walked

in beautiful skin

within the bright shine in my eyes

I realized you reflected

somethin of my own


We all starred at your naked legs

I could hear them thoughts

loud


monstrous

predators

and me?


For a second, no word is spoken

for a moment all shifted

I hated not you

I hated these powerful thoughts

and knowing, you'd play with them too

that spooks me

and there is this unpleasant truth

We hold an undeniable power

in our wombs

In this world

where pushed to play by others' rules

dismantle the bricks

and lurke the equal

it is still your choice


how you play it out

your end of the bargain

in my lies in time solemnly your reflection

thus to speak my choice

of intention

# World in progress

My world

is unique

my world

is devine

this word

I write

So

                                        I shall

                                        write

                                        como me

                                        surja

                                        la boca

My world

is divided

in so many levels

it's a diverse

universe

whole

in itself

My so called human

need

urges

**trained to think**

in answers

as I dance

in the twilight

of their non existence

I fear myself

in power

find rest in fear

itself

I tumble

in the pain

until the worlds

go under

again

*upside down*

*again*

I feel I can

do this

until every new end

beggin-ning

I found something

I lost a while ago

It's the word streaming out

through my blood

again

And again

I see

nothing

but colors

           I dance in the shadows

         of my own imperfections

I dance for myself

in the urge to be free

so majestically

        This moment can't be shared

          But the work

            well done

             flows out

in different tongues

splitted their ends in two

Until the next episode

honestly

I am never done

# In and out

drawn in and out of distractions

lost again in possibilities

designed

to make it hard to pull together

what is wanted stays in dust

locked in the cellar

The key I burry

deep in my soul

in diagonal, so it itches,

and pulls

I'll never be comfortable to stay stuck

it urges me moving

it urges me

to put

one foot

in front

of the other

no matter what

no matter where

I swim like a fish

in waters

I was called

a free soul ones

and I carry the words with me

whenever I hear the birds

sing to me,

I celebrate my rebirth

bath in the morning

## Creators

I see us

breaking

under the pressure.

We are bending

a system

that only holds up

because it bands people

who think like us

Its tools

are made

of such unbending measures

it doesn't want us

and we know it

so we struggle

the only way

to dismantle this house

is to tear it down

brick by brick

is to move in another one

but do it

without moving

no crushing

we do it

brick by brick

we change

while something else arises

ancient, not new

new tools old house

old tools new house

repeat:

I myself am never able to explain it

I am only a spark of it


new tools must be used

new material

recycled in old ways

we think

it breaks us

so we go gentle


we must think


we can't break it


but, with fierce,


The house needs us


there is no home


without the soul



I am reading your work


and I am grateful


we do this

I know now

I am not alone

in this

feeling uncomfortable

unuseful

and

its

only

my fierce

against its tools

that makes it so.

## Careless & Awareness

My feelings

that it's wrong

is most often

the only source

of I have

of knowledge

that there is something going on

You however

are the harm

you don't know

when you don't care

and most often, you don't.

# Critiques prize

Learning objects in one category only

always came uneasy to me

to name objects in categories

One genre of writing

can be [       ] so many things

I accept and listen you call it that way,

in the same way to me

it'll weight more both of it


In diverse themes, I see easily our similari-

ties


to box out the differences only inspires me


in the moment I define an idea

and that doesn't burry or erase its similari-

ties


and proximity to other –the contrary


Communication is at least a two way street

and when I am done communicating

I wonder when that will be

The freedom my way of thinking gifts me

with the freedom to create

while it's up to others to box, to stuff into

their categories,

so my work can be evaluated.

Within my space I wander free

within the others there is a high prize to pay.

**Wenn alle Freien scheinen, reden wir weiter**

Was echt ist liegt in mir

was echt ist liegt in dir

wir müssen nicht einer Meinung sein

um das zu akzeptiern'

Ich brauche auch kein

Territorium

um mein Revier zu markieren.

Das meine ist alles,

was in meinem Schein leuchtet

das meine ist ein

sich ständig Wandelndes

Sein


das gerade

korreliert mit dem Deinen


Wenn all die,

die nicht frei sind,

schreien

im List scheinen

reden wir vielleicht weiter

# To every beloved worker in the educational sector

Believing in myself

talking about myself

is the scariest thing

I have ever done.

If my desire of being free

would not swing with a hundred pounds

against my chest

I'd rather let them be

*You told me I wasn't enough to be what I want to be*

but every moon when the sky heres I am

still quite

*I was just pushing you to be better*

they come and teach again & ask when I'm

feeling brave enough to feel

*I don't think you were*

feel enough to let them free.

*And even if that is true, your words really crushed me & I almost didn't come back because of you. Unlike other students, I haven't been growing up being told that I am brilliant or deserving. If I take a risk and it doesn't work out I don't have a safety net to fall back on. And you will come across others like me, so*

*I just want you to know that as a teacher your words hold a lot of power.*


*I decide you aren't going to be the goal keeper of my dreams*

# I had to write it down_

write it down,

like so many others,

write it down,

so it counts.

I feel & my thoughts

run crazy,

if I don't calm them down

like two freshly lovers,

calming them down.

Like brushing my teeth

running back without spitting

a thought is so precious

and most gone within seconds

how many times

I ran and fell insearch of a pen


Relying on my battery is never an option


I reevaluate craziness

when once I put down to rest

the foggy mood of emptiness,

using the power

of a pencil

to gain my own trust

in stability

and heal

like all pencil healers

in the universe.


I gather my thoughts

participate the overcome

all the damage that calls me

and that has been done

by generations

years and centuries

of abuse

of papers,

of stealing from who man

and ripe the wo man,

thrive a patch

to wom until an

y one doesn't believe in the death of spaces

anymore

I fill spots with ink where

awkwardness occurs,

while we ignore, because

everyone became too inconvenient

for the perfect storyboard,

lost even ourselves _

here and now

[imagine a melodie     playing you space]


Your hurt is in question

 for the love deep down you are seeking.

For the who and the how

your pencil as a weapon,

creates the medicine_

if you learn to swing

it


believing

in your magic.

So, only shoot

with learnings

deep inside.

Get there,

turn on the lights,

shine bride

for this,

let go of the outside,

shine bride

then let the lessons in.


Let the reflection of your own light

be your guide.


Talk to you,

talk to the ones before.

Ask them

Where have you been?

Are you here for more?


Even if there were not there



when you needed them the most.

Grieve for them and for yourself,

if they should be here to protect you,


Every generation

is to overcome

their fears and flaws

of an old one.

Now the scars of wars became human trau-

mas.

Hands important, I say it again

It is okay to grieve.


[pause]


And it is okay to believe.

As long as you leave

space

between believe and faith_

you are able to trace

back your steps

within control and disgrace.

Wind and wind

in circles

like we all

do,

unfold your own myth

like the grandmasters

told us too.

Find your shrine

in

everything you do_


as dirty as it might look

don't mind the outside

don't lose side on your goals.

You never let anyone

dismantle or take it,

for it is in our souls.

The power to love

yourself,

leads you to accept

everybody else.

Don't confuse this burden

in your earthly body


with the projection

of the bodies around you.

Not everybody learned the

true power of self control.

Now_

you love yourself dearly,

the lights around you got a chance

 to shine their light

right back at you_

brightly.


*Mantra*

# In Ehren an May Ayim

„

während noch immer und schon wieder

die einen zerstückelt und verteilt und vertrie-

ben werden

die einen

die immer die anderen sind und waren und

bleiben sollen erklären sich die

eigentlich anderen

noch immer und schon

wieder zu den einzig wahren

erklären uns die eigentlich anderen:

noch immer und schon wieder den krieg

es ist ein blues in Schwarzweiß

1/3 der welt

zertanzt die anderen

2/3 sie feiern in weiß

wir trauern in Schwarz

es ist ein blues in Schwarzweiß es ist ein blues

das wieder vereinigte deutschland

feiert sich wieder 1990

ohne immigrantInnen flüchtlinge jüdische und

schwarze menschen ...

es feiert in intimem kreis

es feiert in weiß

doch es ist ein blues in Schwarzweiß es ist ein

blues

das vereinigte deutschland das vereinigte eu-

ropa die

vereinigten staaten

feiern 1992

500 jahre columbustag

500 jahre vertreibung versklavung und völ-

kermord

in den amerikas

und in asien

und in afrika

1/3 der welt vereinigt sich

gegen die anderen 2/3

im rhythmus von rassismus sexismus und anti-

semitismus

wollen sie uns isolieren unsere geschichte aus-

radieren

oder bis zur unkenntlichkeit

mystifizieren

es ist ein blues in Schwarzweiß es ist ein blues

doch wir wissen bescheid wir wissen be-

scheid

1/3 der menschheit feiert in weiß

2/3 der menschheit macht nicht mit

"

blues in Schwarz und weiß

von

May Ayim

*Quelle: Ayim, May (1995): „blues in Schwarz-*

*weiß". Berlin, Orlanda Frauenverlag.*

# Backwards

Let me have faith

that this is

what I have to do

Give me the strength

that I will do it

I keep going on

even though

against odds


Even though I am asked

and told to be wrong


*I keep going backwards*

# Unlearnings of Love

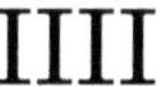

# IIII

## Rollen

Wir stehen auf

und ziehen uns eine Rolle an

Wir nehmen unsere Rolle an

Nehme ich heute das rote

oder das blaue Hemd?

Nach welcher Rolle fühle ich mich

Wir schminken uns

Wir schminken uns

199

unsere Rolle an


*Ich ~~bin~~ eine Frau*

## In diesem Leben


Ich habe einen Begleiter gefunden

einen Bremser

einen Beschleunigungsmodus

einen Patienten

und einen Arzt

ein Ziel

sowie einen Start

meine Medizin

und meine Krankheit

einen Vater

einen Sohn

eine Schwester

einen Geliebten

eine Großmutter

einen Enkel

meinen Mann

und meine Frau

meine Liebe

und meinen Hass

mein Ende

*und meinen Anfang*

# A

Dieses Gefühl zu beschreiben,

ist ein Ding der Unmöglichkeit

und keine der Worte wird dem je gerecht

sein.


Als doch es nicht zu versuchen,

trotz des nicht gerecht werdens

wäre des Künstlers großer Unmut.

Jedes Mal, wenn ich sie in dir suche,

treibt es mich, dir diese Liebe zu er reichen.

Doch sie erreicht uns allein ohne Sinn.


Sie reichen aus, will ich lernen

zu genügen, zu akzeptieren

gilt es mich als Menschenkind


Et ?was verändert sich in mir

im Mensch-sein mit dir

seitdem du in mir bist

körperlich

vergeht die Zeit ganz wunderlich

So, als existiere sie nicht

ohne dich–

ich kann dich riechen,

schmecken, hören, sehen

Ganz so, als seist du hier bei mir

wie eine Hülle um die Raupe

hast du dich schützend um mich gelegt.

Ich möchte,

nur für dich zum Schmetterling werden,

*der erblüht, wenn er dich sieht*

# B

Ganz verliebt

drehen sich Hormone

in meinem Bauch


Mein Magen,

als Antwort

auf mein expandierendes Herz

verarbeitet

tüchtig

was gerade passiert.


Viel zu viele Glücksgefühle,

die alle

nicht befriedigt werden


türmen sich

gen Schleimhäute

wie Fremdkörper –

wenn nicht expandieren,

dann halt ausgeschieden

scheint ihre Mission

und

Miss Hypo und die Zellen beraten

gegen die Störkörper vorzugehen

Wie ein Fehler im System,

sie versuchen mich abzuheben,

doch ich bleibe auf dem Boden

kaum abgehoben

schwebe ich nur ein bisschen

auf den Hormonen-Drogen


Atme tief ein

und erkenne meine Lektionen

mein System wird umgepolt


Grenzenlose Liebe

Miss Jones,

danke

ist kein StÖrling,

es ist das schÖnste Geschenk,

dass frau mir geben kann

Miss Hypo–

weder dagegen ankÄmpfen

aber FÜße

hiergeblieben, verweilen –ein bisschen

vielleicht hilfts ja,

*etwas aufzuschreiben.*

## Shadow work

I know

the times

when

despair

shuffled

my path

rocks

the size of a mountain

wrecked my sight

left nothing but fog

to my dusty eyes

dragged me to war


no way out

but

to

give

in

keep

on going

move

don't

give

in

I leave

my

sent


by

going

my

way

I love

I care

# Let Love be the light

Time is a funny thing

future

past

present


it all gets mixed up


there is only one way to keep it ~~straight~~


is to remember what really matters.

Of course

keeping sight

on what's important

can be hard

.

Sometimes it feels like

we'll always be alone

and the only thing

keeping us

company

is our own pain

.

"We tell ourselves

we are the problem

especially

when things

we can't control

come our way."

That

is

why

we

must

let go

of our pain

and regret


and

remember

who are we fighting for

These are the ones we love.

let that be the light

that guides you

through the most treacherous of times

and the darkest

of nights

# Mi t e **rror**

It's amazing

how far

we'll go

to hide our true selves from the world


perhaps

its

because

we don't

want them to know

how much

we really care for them


what is funny

because we'd do

anything for them.

We travel incredible distances

We even fight monsters

for them.


I suppose it is scary to admit that you need

people.

Some say having friends is a great liability,

a weakness


After all

what greater pain is there

then to lose someone you love

or worse

someone you love, has left you behind.


I guess


that's why we feel the need to hide away

and protect ourselves


So we put on

a mask

It is not hard to understand

why

what's hard is knowing

that sometimes

the mask

is

who

we

really

are

–

**sex education**

# Avatar 5

It was from this oasis

that the tribe looked up in the sky and learned to bend the water

by watching the moon



push


and


pull

the tides of the tides.

And so they believed

their lives come from the spirit of the ocean

while their power come from the spirit of the

moon

We don't have to be afraid of our pain

*we just have to decide what we are going to do*

*with it.*

**Yes,**

susurro con la vibración

de nos magnetismo

I fancy you.

I desire your

come to my,

when I come

Right now

in the humble illusion

of your soul

touching mine.

And it keeps me goin'

it moves my body

in waves.

Inspires my

loving self

desiring self

in beauty

**with unity.**

# faith vs believe

You can hear the same message a thousand times,

but it is you who has to collect the cure

honor it

keep it

*safe*

(Y)our love is greater than fear.

deine Liebe ist größer als Angst.

(Y)our love is stronger than uncertainty.

deine Liebe ist stärker als Ungewissheit.


(Y)our love is deeper than hate.

deine Liebe ist tiefer als Hass.


You shall

Love your neighbor as you love yourself


yourself

yourself

yourself


Love begins in the heart, can you feel your heart?

**Do you have faith in your believes?**

# Let m.e go

in the end

of trying

you and I

if anything

we should go back to

being friends

for you can't be easy

around me

.

I am done

playing dumb.

For you can't ever own me.

I am as free

**as water runs towards the sea.**

**Two spirits**

In meinem Körper

da wohnen zwei.

Es ist schwierig zu beschreiben.

In meinem Herzen

da wohnen zwei.

Ich fühle mich oft entzweit,

denn die Welt meint

täglich

sie zu ent-scheiden

.

So als könnte die Sonne untergehn'

ohne danach den Mond zu sehn'.

# Love for the abuser

I have always learned the hard way

As my journey has started ruff & with pain

The intruders have put seeds in my brain

of how s/he cards lay fo r eign my life.


Now from time to time

when thoughts of sabotage arise

I come to realize

that in this journey of mine

I mostly put energy

in unlearning what previously

I held hostage.


Would I have

been ready to identify

the intruders from an early age

Would I have been more terrified

Could I have stand been isolated?

Here the crux is set–

I tolerated,

I imitated,

I impersonated

I loved them

I learned to appreciate.

the bully

the drug

the abuser

the controller


Now

I do not appreciate your tight grab.

I appreciate values

I value honesty

I honestly dislike your controlled anger

I do like myself

Myself just didn't believe it yet


*until I myself stopped believing you*

## Therapy is Love

I think

you shouldn't

block out

all these emotions

,

Because that is how

heartbreaks

become unsolved

and turn

into

something bitter


It is really important

that you feel all those feelings.


As

much

as

they

hurt

.

sex education

"He touched me. N. abused me. I don't think I am ok."

"I think I need some help but I am scared!"


"I don't seem to be able to stay in one place too long. I am scared that if I stop moving & start properly talking about what happened then it might catch up with me

and I won't be able to pretend that I am okay anymore."

**Sex education**

## Let it bleed out

I am confused

you are

emotionally coercive,

but so have I.

Your deep eyes

resembled therefore

so well

with mine.

It's threatening

I let that detail

slip

so quick & eager

to ignore

all red flags

only to hold on

to this one connection

a bond

beyond

boundaries

bent to bed.

So here I am

again

sad

and all bled

out.

Lilijanea J.

# No

The word

No.

is so powerful

in many ways.


It brings me

Shame

when I think it


Anger

When I say it

Sadness

when I don't.


*Intersectionality*

*nach loslassen*

Lilijanea J.

# kommt loslassen

## Out of the box

Yes, most people

will put you in boxes

write on it

what suits them

or whatever they can

in their thinking

is limited.

Look for those

who don't.

        Stay where

        you don't have

        to bent

            But feel confidence

              to use o  space

            for revealing your spirit o

N o one

c a n hold you together.

B u t there are beautiful clips

to complete the wonderful puzzle

I s

*y o u*

## Community Wise

"I know a lot of you think what I just said is sinful & that I need to pray for forgiveness, but you're wrong.

My heart is torn,

because

I am

in a position

where

I have to choose

between

whether to hide my truth

& live in pain

or be honest

and

lose my community.


*sex education*


I keep getting told,

that I have to wait

and be patient,

but I'm tired of waiting.

And I love myself too much to not tell my

truth."

"Things have to chance,

because people like us

are not going anywhere.

I know that the world can be harsh,

but you are not alone

We need you here with us.

**Shall we bring you home?"**

## Grieve

I hate this pain

because I can't grieve

with your presence


on not having you anymore

never had never will

it's not in my cards


The pain is stuck with me

like I am stuck with your identity

for evermore

Have you ever felt that before?

Shame

shame

shame

Oh
that poor thing

What's worse

the pity

or

the shame?

If you understand

you understand

solidarity

you might get

you yourself

*Dignity*

## Your decision

## My decision

I got asked

once

or twice

in my life

time

to make a decision

on a destination

for somebody else,

again

and

again


I state

if you are too afraid

to decide

for yourself

I defiantly rooted you to think it through

until the end


and I won't pretend

I

can

give

you

just my hand

I refuse

on

a responsibility

on me

that I could never carry


I may see my desires

clearly

but not your destination

not your destiny

i'ss not up to me to see


I'd rather go solo

than drag someone along

It has to be bold

it has to be all

So,

I can't hold

the ball alone

I pass it on

come on,

turn it on

bring it

around

I cheer

***it's your turn***

# Crush ed

Deine gelockten Haare

und dein schelmisches Lächeln


deine Unschuldigen Hände

deine Klarheit in den Augen


Dein behütetes Nest

in dem du noch immer brütend sitzt


Du, deine Gaben, deine schlauen Augen

die sich brüsten, sie zu beschützen

"

I think you loved him

&

you let him go


so now you don't have anyone left to love

but yourself

"

# **para el niño feliz**

Si tuviera lata

para captar mis lágrimas

y así enseñartelas

cuando vuelvas


supieras de todos mis días

que te pensé amando

y que las lágrimas corridas no mienten


Tus pecas eran los coordinantes

que en las noches

todavía me senalan

el camino a la alegría

tu me bailaste una canción

que jamás olvidaría


me sonríe por siempre
el niño feliz
Me coquetean pequitas
me juegan a salir


De mi cuna


cansada
y por miedo al fuego
en vez de coqueta
me hago Einsiedler
y cuando no mires
me escondo otra vez


dentro de mi cueva
anhelandote como huevona

Lilijanea J.

# Abschied von einem toxischen Mann

Der Grund

warum

ich dich verlies

ist dein fehlender Respekt

Die einzige Frage

die mir mal durch den Kopf ging

ist ob deine Frau weiß

dass du vor einem Nein nicht zurückscheust

Deine Unehrlichkeit

Deine Überheblichkeit

entriss

jede MÖglichkeit

von ewiger Verbundenheit


Ich bin gegangen

damit du's weißt

weil keine Liebe

dein Gift ge heilt

hat

# La respuesta de Sandalio a Ernesto

## Güemes

Ahora sé

que el amor sin solidaridad

es egoísmo

Y también he comprendido

que la solidaridad

deviene premiosa y autocomplaciente

si le falte el compromiso


Y este se vuelve orgulloso

cuando le faltan

sus dos amigos

## In the heart of a princess

## there is always truth

I see beautiful things

not perfect

is

what makes them so beautiful


Ich sehe Augen

und ich liebe es

ich sehe suchende Augen

liebende Augen

wollende Augen

begehrende Augen

befriedigte Augen


Der Moment

wenn du dich in Augen verlieren kannst

für diesen Moment

ist das Leben

lebenswert


Für einen Augenblick

bedeutet die Welt alles

und nichts

ist unmöglicher, als nicht in dem Moment

zu leben

Ich sehe Augen

& ich sehe Seelen

Ich sehe sie an

und manchmal halte ich schwer aus–

manchmal muss ich wegschauen.

Es gibt so viele schöne Dinge


Ja, ich möcht' nie wieder wegschauen

Ich will sie alle sammeln,

diese schönen Momente


Mich stets erinnern

an die schönen Augen

in denen ich mich zu verlieren liebe

Hinzuschauen heißt loszulassen

# Miedo

no tengas miedo

de que se vayan

ni temes que vengan


al venir

pregúntales

que algo irán buscando

abre tu corazón

para ver que es


No tengas miedo

de la verdad

no te cierres

por tu miedo


Abre los ojos

para ver

abre tu corazón

para escuchar


no huyas de lo que es

concéntrate en lo verdadero

o

accepta lo que hay


que es lo que ves

lo que escuchas

lo que sientes

# compañer@ de mi alma

No se necesita a otra persona

para vivir el mismo diario día tras otro


Pero tener a una persona que te ilumina la

tarde

fuera de lo cotidiano

para escaparte de la rutina de la vida


que te saca sonrisas y que te lleva a la felici-

dad

lejos de la a veces agotadora realidad


esa me parece algo que vale la pena

mantenerla para siempre

.

## un Difícil adiós

Ya no hay nada que decir

estás a mil kilómetros

la barrera dentro de mi

te lo ensena a cada paso


La pregunta de siempre sigue aquí

que sería y que puede haber sido

por que el amor no alcanzó

a superar la falta de respeto

porque no merezco esto


Aquella no era nuestra canción

no evidente en su día

no obstante aquí que terminó

veo que dulzura la mezclé con perfección


Mañana despertaré sin ti

lloraré pero feliz

advertiré en el abandono

la pureza falleció en tu ser deshonesto

# Wer früher stirbt ist länger tot

Zwischenmenschliches

war

noch

nie

leicht

die geborenen Umstände

nie leicht zu überwinden


Das Leben anzunehmen, wie es kommt

ist eine Lebensaufgabe geblieben


Trotz alle dem glücklich zu bleiben

Bei mir bin ich, wenn ich nicht gerade dabei

bin

mein Glück irgendwo anders zu suchen

Lilijanea J.

# Manchmal schaff ichs zu lassen – das Glück

## dass da ist

und das Leben dass schön sein kann

## die Worte finden

...ich such ja schon


doch

ich finde die Worte nicht

dir zu erklären

wie ich mich fühl


umso ich versuche

diese Gedanken in Worten zu gebären

mehr & mehr verliere ich mich

abwärts Spiral-

Gefühl Richtung Machtlosigkeit


Am Ende scheint es so klar

ich möchte mit dir sein

Nur in der Nähe

sind meine Gefühle so unvereint

Lilijanea J.

Im Eifer des Gefechts

kommt mir Dein & Mein

vor

wie ein unÜberwindbarer Meilenstein

**Fear ruled love**

in possession of class


So, you asked me

Why

I feel insecure

between you and me

and her

sharing a space

I tell you

behind closed doors

You two share

a light fear less

a proper ego in time flesh

of no responsibility.


Whereas I am never going to be

that lightly

you run free & blurred with headache.

But you think you didn't chose

to be un-free

that is what makes me angry

I chose constantly to break free


And you

so many times

choose ignorancy


The difference and source of my distrust

is

that you can always decide to

go back to your safety bed

where everything is laid out for yourself


Don't take it the wrong way

don't put it on me


I am happy

you have safety

I would want to have it


but when I turn around

there is a bunch of angry people

that didn't get enough

like myself

an I have to meditate it

constantly

.

When you two lough

I think of the things

you and I will never have

and what you nor I will never be

You might feel for me

I hope – everything but sorry

but we will never share in silence

the carry I burden


For you may learn to be an ally

to me and 'break free'

but I can't help it, I see the chains

in you, that remind

the hold

of me

# Im Schatten der Unsicherheiten

Eine Stimme in mir

ich wills nicht verbergen,

sie flüstert in der Stille

ich verdiene es nicht

geliebt zu werden.


Der Unterschied

zwischen dir und mir

mein Schatz

ist

ich brauche niemanden

an meiner Seite

um zu verfälschen

dass es so nicht gehen kann


Ich gestehe es mir

lieber so lange ein

bis sich die Angst

verwandelt

in Sonnenschein


Wenn du bei mir sein willst

trotz der Schatten

lade ich dich ein

ich mache meine Sachen

du machst deine Sachen


doch frag mich nicht,

nach Zuspruch

als Anspruch

Ich gebe ihn gerne von allein

wenn ich fühle, dass er echt ist.

## My hormones raise

they gather

to evolve

the egg

my temperature rises

I cant hold it

my fingers

vibrate

reaching for fulfillment

my desire

pictures everyone

to my pleasure

I urge to please


I urge to fuck

at these times

I fuck the best


Don't underestimate

the power my body inherits

don't wrongly praise love

when desire inhabits

# Reborn

What rises in such waves

is known to be reborn

so

its death

is inevitable

.

be still and you can watch her

**transformation into various life forms.**

Lilijanea J.

# Begegnung des Abschieds

Ihr Haar war schwarz

ihre Stimme zart

bröckelig wie einst die Fassade

am Haus

still vor sich hin wimmerte

sie bangte um ihren Willen

der längst verflogen war

mit den Geschichten

die allein ihr dasein schmückten


Gefangen im Wahn

Sinnlos umher

ging ihre Seele

suchte nach einer Frage

die Sinn machte.

Zu mir wandte sie sich

sie sah mir Fülle im Herzen

wollte sie ein Stück ab haben?

Sie traute sich

Nichts

zu sagen

und umging den Preis

einer Wahrhaftigkeit

in Offenbarung

im Geschenk

meiner Ungewissheit

sah ich

wer ich bekommen war

Sie zwang mich zur Umkehr

doch ich ließ sie zurück

Ich schmiedete mein

Sie schmiedete ihr

ein Moment

in Stille

un

Glück

und

beide

fragten sich

entzweit

haben

oder

**sein**

# A few words

May I introduce some of me through this book, you are holding dear right now. It is a hell of a ride -this journey we call life.

And we can even live in heaven on earth. Not in a made-up farytail, but in this magical world, where really everything is connected.

And like my father said - everybody is an art.ist,

So thank you art.ist, teacher, preacher, teenager, pensionist, wor- ker, creator, reader...

I am so glad you are with me on this journey. That means you and I are going together through a path of growth, resiliance and independence

while growing in passion, love and unity, because community is every- thing. We are never better off alone,

take my hand.

# Hand to paper

*If one day this book gets old and you don't feel like reading it anymore, pass it on to the next bookshelf with love. You never know, whom it might inspire or help.*

*If you want to know it all, read this book like you can't wait to get to know every inch of me.*

*If you want to get only sparks of inspiration, I recommend you to read this collection, like I read ‚The evolution of a Girl'. We writers are tempted to flow in inspiration, and some readers, like I, tend looping deep into a book, getting really absorbed. I find that poetry should not be consumed, but thought of. A poem can leave you a mark in the long run – if you let it sink in.*

*When, after a while reading page after page, I feel the text merged into one big bubble of nothing much new, I abandon the book for a while*

*and come back to it, opening it ran-
domly wherever I feel my thumb to
stop fanning it. This was the page I
would read. I guess that is why I
worked on an index and chapters as
well – so you can close the book,
find a nice title and go again.*

*I would never abandon this way of
reading poetry afterwards.*

*I also experienced that I have been
given various books, which I wasn't
supposed to read yet. So comes, sometimes, I have books up my win-
dowshelf, in my closet, or with a
friend for years. I know I will read
the book eventually when I am ready
and then the day comes, when I remember them. I go back, get them out of
the closet, or dust them from the
webs that where spinned by my A' friends at the window and emerse in the
journey of a new teacher, storyteller
and companion .. I never come back
the same.*

*You may have noticed that I write in 3-4 languages – don't let that scare you in any way. I invite you in this series to flow in your soulful perceptions, more then in analytical thinking. I encourage you to let the future of multilingualism flow in you for as much as possible.*

*Enjoy the ride.*

*I am proud to have become a part in your journey.*

*Love, L*

# **further work**

## **Publications**

from the series:

*Words that can be spoken out loud*


- Reflexions

- Space(s)


Write me for shorter booklets of this series

as a gift or for your curiuos mind

- Only German edition (deutsche Version für Freunde und Familie aus Deutschland) (30 Seiten)

- Unlearnings of love (40 pages)

- Active Thought (35 pages)

**lilijaneaj@gmail.com**

Lilijanea J.

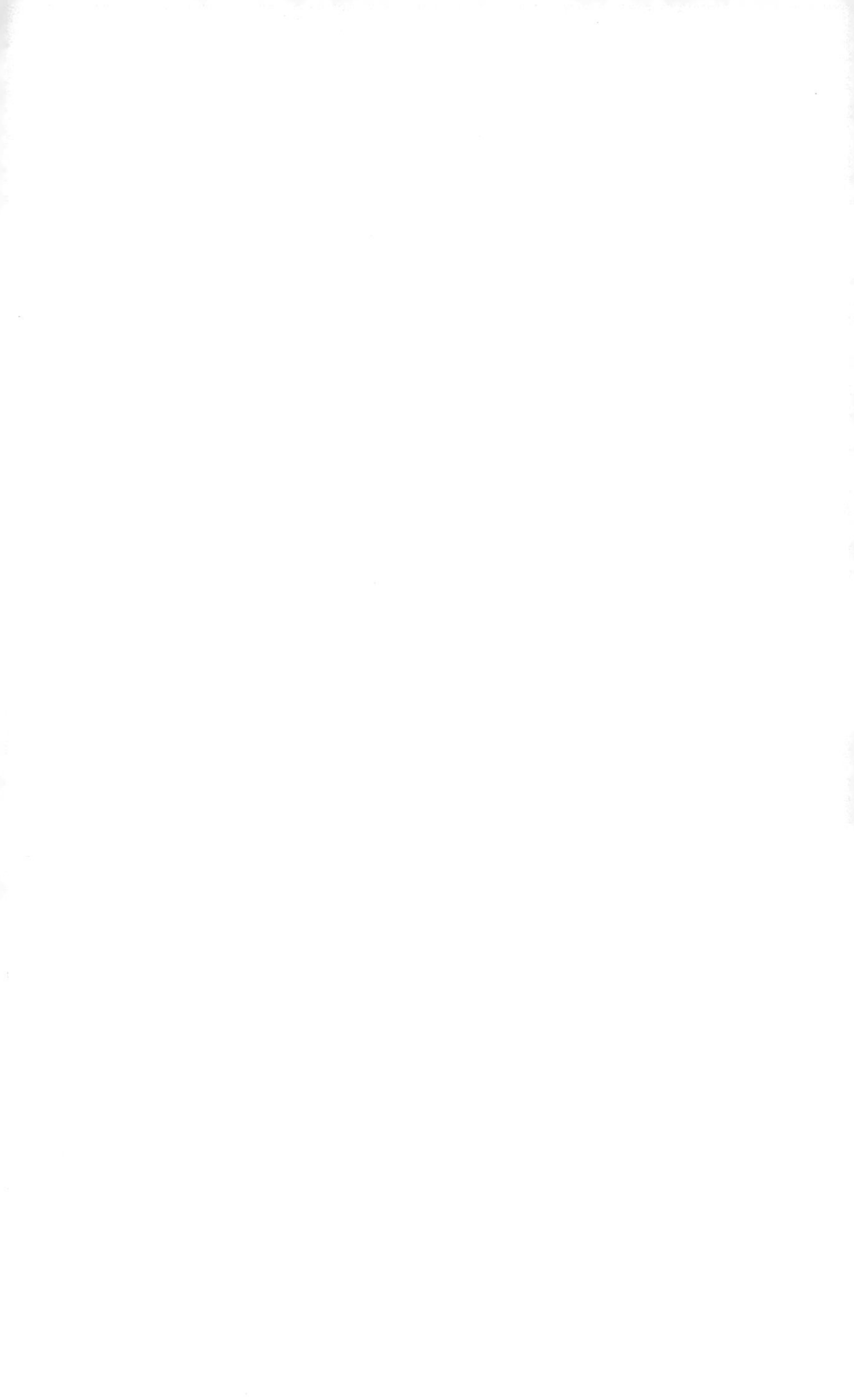